George Rogers Clark

American General

Colonial Leaders

Lord Baltimore
English Politician and Colonist

Benjamin Banneker
American Mathematician and Astronomer

Sir William Berkeley
Governor of Virginia

William Bradford
Governor of Plymouth Colony

Jonathan Edwards
Colonial Religious Leader

Benjamin Franklin
American Statesman, Scientist, and Writer

Anne Hutchinson
Religious Leader

Cotton Mather
Author, Clergyman, and Scholar

Increase Mather
Clergyman and Scholar

James Oglethorpe
Humanitarian and Soldier

William Penn
Founder of Democracy

Sir Walter Raleigh
English Explorer and Author

Caesar Rodney
American Patriot

John Smith
English Explorer and Colonist

Miles Standish
Plymouth Colony Leader

Peter Stuyvesant
Dutch Military Leader

George Whitefield
Clergyman and Scholar

Roger Williams
Founder of Rhode Island

John Winthrop
Politician and Statesman

John Peter Zenger
Free Press Advocate

Revolutionary War Leaders

John Adams
Second U.S. President

Samuel Adams
Patriot

Ethan Allen
Revolutionary Hero

Benedict Arnold
Traitor to the Cause

John Burgoyne
British General

George Rogers Clark
American General

Lord Cornwallis
British General

Thomas Gage
British General

King George III
English Monarch

Nathanael Greene
Military Leader

Nathan Hale
Revolutionary Hero

Alexander Hamilton
First U.S. Secretary of the Treasury

John Hancock
President of the Continental Congress

Patrick Henry
American Statesman and Speaker

William Howe
British General

John Jay
First Chief Justice of the Supreme Court

Thomas Jefferson
Author of the Declaration of Independence

John Paul Jones
Father of the U.S. Navy

Thaddeus Kosciuszko
Polish General and Patriot

Lafayette
French Freedom Fighter

James Madison
Father of the Constitution

Francis Marion
The Swamp Fox

James Monroe
American Statesman

Thomas Paine
Political Writer

Molly Pitcher
Heroine

Paul Revere
American Patriot

Betsy Ross
American Patriot

Baron Von Steuben
American General

George Washington
First U.S. President

Anthony Wayne
American General

Famous Figures of the Civil War Era

John Brown
Abolitionist

Jefferson Davis
Confederate President

Frederick Douglass
Abolitionist and Author

Stephen A. Douglas
Champion of the Union

David Farragut
Union Admiral

Ulysses S. Grant
Military Leader and President

Stonewall Jackson
Confederate General

Joseph E. Johnston
Confederate General

Robert E. Lee
Confederate General

Abraham Lincoln
Civil War President

George Gordon Meade
Union General

George McClellan
Union General

William Henry Seward
Senator and Statesman

Philip Sheridan
Union General

William Sherman
Union General

Edwin Stanton
Secretary of War

Harriet Beecher Stowe
Author of Uncle Tom's Cabin

James Ewell Brown Stuart
Confederate General

Sojourner Truth
Abolitionist, Suffragist, and Preacher

Harriet Tubman
Leader of the Underground Railroad

George Rogers Clark

American General

Michael Burgan

Arthur M. Schlesinger, jr.
Senior Consulting Editor

Chelsea House Publishers

Philadelphia

CHELSEA HOUSE PUBLISHERS
Editor-in-Chief Sally Cheney
Director of Production Kim Shinners
Production Manager Pamela Loos
Art Director Sara Davis
Production Editor Diann Grasse

Staff for *GEORGE ROGERS CLARK*
Editor Sally Cheney
Associate Art Director Takeshi Takahashi
Series Design Keith Trego
Cover Design 21st Century Publishing and Communications, Inc.
Picture Researcher Pat Holl
Layout 21st Century Publishing and Communications, Inc.

The Chelsea House World Wide Web address is
http://www.chelseahouse.com

First Printing
1 3 5 7 9 8 6 4 2

Library of Congress Cataloging-in-Publication Data

Burgan, Michael.
    George Rogers Clark / Michael Burgan.
        p. cm. — (Revolutionary War leaders)
    Includes bibliographical references and index.
    ISBN 0-7910-6394-1 (hc : alk. paper) — ISBN 0-7910-6395-X
    (pbk. : alk. paper)
      1. Clark, George Rogers, 1752-1818—Juvenile literature. 2. Generals
    —United States—Biography—Juvenile literature. 3. United States.
    Continental Army—Biography—Juvenile literature. 4. Virginia—
    Militia—Biography—Juvenile literature. 5. Northwest, Old—History
    —Revolution, 1775-1783—Campaigns—Juvenile literature. 6. United
    States—History—Revolution, 1775-1783—Campaigns—Juvenile
    literature. 7. Frontier and pioneer life—Northwest, Old—Juvenile
    literature. [1. Clark, George Rogers, 1752-1818. 2. Generals. 3. United
    States—History—Revolution, 1775-1783.] I. Title. II. Series.

E207.C5 B87 2001
973.3'3'092—dc21
[B]   2001028527

Publisher's Note: In Colonial and Revolutionary War America,
there were no standard rules for spelling, punctuation, capitaliza-
tion, or grammar. Some of the quotations that appear in the Colonial Leaders and Revolutionary War Leaders series come from
original documents and letters written during this time in history.
Original quotations reflect writing inconsistencies of the period.

Contents

Frontiersmen lived in log cabins, such as the one shown in this painting by F. F. Palmer in Utica, New York.

Young Frontiersman

I n the 18th century, large **plantations** that grew tobacco and other crops stretched over the Virginia countryside. The plantation owners were the most important people in the colony.

John and Ann Clark owned a farm, too. It was small, compared to the grand plantations. The Clarks farmed 400 acres of land in Albemarle County, near the Blue Ridge Mountains. The family's first home sat near a spring. It was inside this cabin that red-headed George Rogers Clark was born on November 19, 1752.

The Clark farm was on the **frontier,** about 100

miles from Williamsburg, Virginia's capital at the time. At one time, most settlers in Virginia lived near the Chesapeake Bay. Slowly, more families moved further out, searching for farmland. As the settlers headed west, they inched closer to the lands owned by Native Americans.

Conflicts between American settlers and Indians would play a role in George's later life.

The Ohio River flowed through vast areas of wilderness west of the Clark farm. Few American settlers had seen this land, sometimes called the "Ohio country." Various Native American tribes lived on this land and beyond, including the Shawnee, Miami, and Iroquois.

Many people saw the

George was not the only American hero to come from Abelmarle County. On a neighboring farm, the Jefferson family had a son named Thomas. Years later, Thomas Jefferson wrote the Declaration of Independence, and then went on to become the third president of the United States.

Within George's family, five of the six Clark sons fought during the Revolutionary War. The sixth son, William, was too young to fight, but he won fame as an explorer. In 1804, he and Meriwether Lewis traveled across the Rocky Mountains to the Pacific Northwest.

value of the Ohio country. French trappers roamed this land, looking for furs they could send back to Europe. The leaders of England wanted to control the Ohio country, so they could expand their empire. American colonists thought the lands could one day be turned into productive farms.

The Native Americans of the Ohio country did not want any Europeans on their land. They realized, though, that they could not drive the Europeans away. The French seemed less of a threat to their lands, so many tribes became friendly with them. Other tribes chose to support the English and the colonists.

Small battles sometimes broke out between the Europeans and their Native American neighbors. In 1756 these **skirmishes** turned into a war between France and England. Today this war is called the French and Indian War or the Seven Years' War. During the war, Indians loyal to France sometimes attacked colonists living on the Virginia frontier. In 1757, George

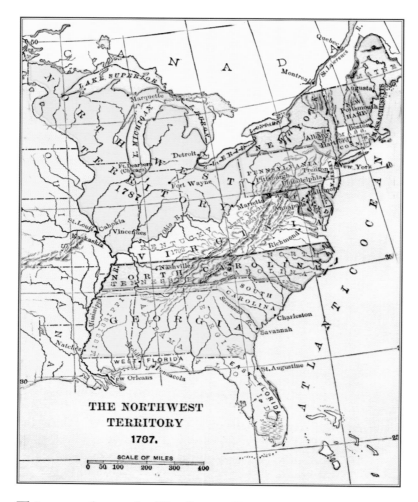

This map shows the Northwest Territory, which was the site of conflicts between American settlers and the Native Americans.

and his family headed east to avoid those attacks and settled in Caroline County.

George was the second Clark son, and he

eventually had four more brothers. For a time, George and his brother Jonathan went to a school run by their uncle, Donald Robertson. They lived with their mother's father, John Rogers, so they could be close to the school.

At first, George was not the best student. But George liked to read and eventually did better in school. He showed an interest in history and geography, and he loved to study nature. This interest in plants and animals helped George when he returned to the frontier.

On the family farm, George learned how to plant different crops. By 15, he had his own plot of land, and he made money selling what he raised. George's grandfather Rogers also taught him how to **survey**. This was an important skill on the frontier, as people needed to know the boundaries of property as they settled new land.

George's goal was to find a large piece of land and start his own plantation. After the French and Indian War, more Americans headed west.

Some wanted to claim land and sell it later at a huge profit. Others, like George, sought to clear the land and farm it.

One area the Americans explored was Kentucky. The Ohio River formed its northern border, and the Kentucky River flowed nearby. Daniel Boone, the famous frontiersman, was one of the first Americans to explore this region. Boone and others came even though the English government did not want American colonists to settle west of the Appalachian Mountains.

In 1772, George left Caroline County to begin his search for land. Packing his surveyor tools, he traveled to Fort Pitt, in present-day Pittsburgh. From there he sailed down the Ohio River and reached what is now West Virginia. A few months later, George returned, describing the beautiful land and wildlife of the "back country." The explorers had avoided any skirmishes with Native Americans and had seen only one European settlement during their travels.

Daniel Boone was one of the first frontiersmen to explore the wilderness of Kentucky. His adventures became famous, and he appeared as the subject of many books and several movies.

By late summer, George was ready to return down the Ohio River. This time his father went with him, along with four friends. The group landed about 40 miles south of Wheeling, Virginia. George claimed a stretch of land near a stream and began to clear away the trees. His friend James Higgins stayed with him, while the others returned to Caroline County.

In a letter to his father, George wrote that his work was going well, and he had received an offer "of a very considerable sum" for his land. George also made money surveying land for the new settlers who came to the region. After setting up his farm, George traveled back to his family's home during the summer of 1773. In the fall, he returned to his land to harvest his corn.

Up to that point, George had no trouble with Native Americans. But as more Americans settled along the Ohio River, tensions rose. Many Americans thought poorly of the Indians, calling them "savages" and believing they prevented settlers from claiming land. The Indians disliked the Americans for settling on their hunting grounds. The settlers were ruining

the Indians' way of life. The two sides sometimes fought each other. If one side attacked a
village, the other responded with killings of
its own.

It would not be long before George faced
the threat of war with the Native Americans.

This map of Kentucky was drawn from observations made by surveyors during colonial times.

On to Kentucky

The settlers in the Ohio Valley could not prevent war with the Native Americans forever. Both sides distrusted each other and had already carried out terrible raids and killings. In the spring of 1774, George joined Captain Michael Cresap, who had experience fighting the Indians, and other Americans on some of these raids against Shawnee Indians. Shortly after, an attack on an Indian chief's family led to full war.

Tachnechdorus was an Iroquois chief. He was more commonly known as John Logan. The Iroquois of the Ohio Valley were mostly friendly with the outsiders coming into the region. Then a group of traders attacked Logan's hunting camp along Yellow Creek. The chief was away during the attack, when he returned, he found all his relatives dead. Logan wanted revenge, and he prepared his warriors for battle. A Shawnee Indian Chief called Cornstalk also joined Logan's forces.

Soon, settlers in the Ohio country fled the frontier. Some headed to Fort Pitt for safety. In Virginia, the governor, Lord Dunmore, prepared to fight Logan and his men. In May, he named George a captain in the Virginia **militia**, the army that defended the colony. Dunmore called upon about 3,000 soldiers to fight the Indians in what was later called "Dunmore's War."

In August, George took part in a raid against the Shawnee. A few months later, half of Dunmore's forces defeated Logan and Cornstalk at a spot called Point Pleasant. The Indians asked the Virginians for peace. Logan sent a message to Dunmore, explaining how the loss of his family had driven him to fight. The chief

Shown in this sketch by Karl Bodmer are various articles of clothing and other items used by American Indians in the 1700s.

wrote, "There runs not a drop of my blood in the veins of any living creature." Still, Logan accepted his defeat, and the Shawnee agreed to stay north of the Ohio River. Peace came to the Ohio Valley–for a little while at least.

As George fought in the back country, other important events were taking place outside Virginia. The American colonists were unhappy about the new taxes the British imposed, especially on tea. In December 1773, some angry residents of Boston threw hundreds of crates of tea into Boston Harbor. This "Boston Tea Party" led the British to pass new laws restricting freedom in the colonies. Now, many Patriots, the Americans who opposed British rule, were calling for changes.

George was not yet involved in these political affairs. He was still looking for land in the Ohio Valley. During Dunmore's War, he heard more about the region of Kentucky. The settlers there had fought with the Virginians against Logan. George reached the settlement of Harrodsburg in 1775, after setting off down the Ohio River from Wheeling.

It didn't take long for George to fall in love with the beautiful scenery of Kentucky. He came to survey land for settlers and to claim some for himself. But no one knew for sure who controlled

The colonists protested Great Britain's tea tax by throwing overboard crates of tea from boats docked in Boston Harbor. The Boston Tea Party led to even more laws imposed on the colonists by the British.

the land George and the others wanted. Even after George made the journey to the Virginia capital of Williamsburg in the fall of 1775, hoping to find out who truly controlled Kentucky, he still had no clear answers.

George planned out the next step for the settlers. As he later wrote, the Kentuckians could "establish an independent government and by giving away a large part of the lands . . . we could not only gain a large number of inhabitants but in large measure protect them." Or they could send someone to Virginia and ask to become part of that colony.

George returned to Harrodsburg in the spring of 1776. He was a confident leader of the settlement. Acting on his own, he called a town meeting to discuss his ideas for Kentucky's future. But even before George arrived at the meeting, the settlers made their own decision about what they should do. The Kentuckians voted to ask Virginia to accept their lands as a new county. They also chose George and John Gabriel Jones to take this request to the Virginia Assembly, the part of the government that made the colony's laws.

By now, the American Revolution had begun. American and British troops had clashed

**The American Revolution began in April 1775.
Patriots were fighting to gain independence from
Great Britain. George was on the frontier when
the fighting started.**

in both northern and southern colonies. In
Philadelphia, George's friend, Thomas Jefferson,
was preparing to write the Declaration of Independence. And on the frontier, the British were

asking their Indian **allies** to attack American settlers. George knew his ride to Virginia would be especially dangerous.

Eager to reach Williamsburg quickly, George and John set out alone. This, George later admitted, was a mistake. On the road, they soon saw signs of Indians nearby. The two men moved slowly, often through heavy rain. All around them they heard the popping of Indian guns. They finally came to a deserted fort. George convinced John to wait at the fort for another traveling party coming from Kentucky. The two men waited with their guns loaded and ready to fire, in case of an Indian attack. To their relief, the

Tachnechdorus led a group of western Iroquois called the Mingo. His mother was believed to be French, and Tachnechdorus tried to have good relations with all white people. He took the name "Logan" from an Englishman who became his friend. After the **slaughter** of his family, however, Logan swore to kill 10 Americans for every Indian who had died.

When he lost Dunmore's War, Logan wrote a speech called "Logan's Lament," which was published by Thomas Jefferson. Logan noted how hard he had worked for peace and how his good work had been ignored.

only people who came to the fort were a few Americans. George and John finished their journey traveling with them.

By the time the Kentuckians reached Virginia, the assembly had ended for the summer. John left for North Carolina to help fight some Cherokee who were attacking Americans. George decided to wait in Virginia until the assembly met again. He also found gunpowder for the settlers in Kentucky. They would need the powder to defend themselves from Indian attacks. George could not afford to pay to ship the powder, so the Virginia government finally agreed to send it to Pittsburgh. George then sent a letter home. He told the settlers they should bring the kegs of powder down the river from Pittsburgh to Kentucky.

In the fall, the Virginia Assembly met again. John returned to help George present the Kentuckians' request. Some Virginia politicians opposed making Kentucky part of Virginia. But in the end, the assembly gave its permission.

George then learned that his letter about the

gunpowder had not reached Kentucky. He knew how important the powder was for the settlers, so he headed for Pittsburgh. With just a handful of men, he planned to sail the kegs to Kentucky.

In Pittsburgh, George sensed that the violence on the frontier was about to explode. "I found the Indians to be fully prepared for war in the spring," he later wrote. Some Indians at Fort Pitt acted friendly, but George believed they were spies. As he prepared to sail down the Ohio River, George thought the Indians would try to attack him and his men.

George managed to safely reach Kentucky. But Indians were in pursuit. George instructed his men to hide the kegs of gunpowder. The small force then set out on foot. He planned to go to Harrodsburg and come back for the kegs with a larger group of armed men. On the trip, George met four settlers. They told him that a group of armed Kentuckians led by Colonel John Todd was nearby. If George could find these troops, they could help bring the gunpowder to Harrodsburg.

George went ahead to try to find Todd, while John and some other men remained in the woods. A short time later, Todd came upon John. The men decided they would go get the gunpowder without waiting for George to return. Before long, however, Todd and the others were **ambushed** by Shawnee warriors. John was killed, and several other men were taken prisoner. The prisoners did not mention the hidden gunpowder.

On January 2, 1777, a group of about 30 men left Harrodsburg to get the gunpowder. This time the settlers avoided the Indians and brought the powder back to town. George's mission to Virginia had ended successfully. Kentucky was now part of Virginia, which was now a state, not a British colony. And the Kentuckians had their **crucial** gunpowder. George had taken the lead in both actions. He was about to play an even larger role in defending his frontier home.

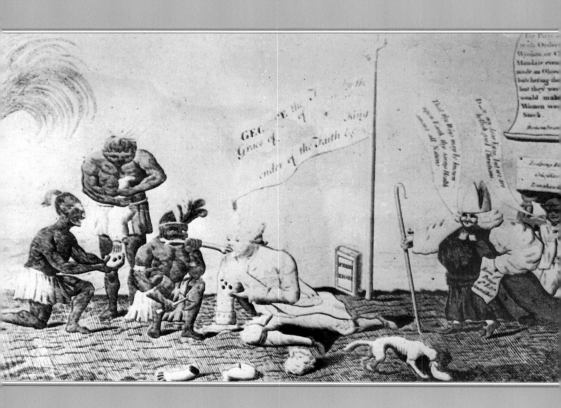

This British cartoon criticizes the king's use of Indians during war in America.

War in the Northwest

At the start of the American Revolution, the British had almost no troops in the Ohio River Valley. Their main fort in the Northwest was in Detroit. This fort was far north of the other forts and settlements of the region. The British counted on help from the Native Americans in the Northwest to battle the Americans. To recruit this aid, the British offered supplies and gifts.

Relations between the British and Native Americans had not started well in the Northwest. Most Indian nations were loyal to the French. But after the British victory in the French and Indian

War, the Indians and the British tried to get along. The American colonists were the biggest threat to the Indians. The frontiersmen often showed their hatred of the Indians and were prepared to kill for their land.

The leader of the British forces in Detroit was Lieutenant Governor Henry Hamilton. Before the American Revolution, Hamilton had tried to limit Indian attacks on American settlers. But in June 1777, Hamilton was told by Great Britain to encourage the Indians to attack the Americans. Soon after this, Hamilton was nicknamed "the Hair-Buyer." George Rogers Clark and others believed he paid the Indians for scalps they took from the Americans.

The Indians of Kentucky had not waited for Hamilton's order to attack. In March 1777, a group of Shawnee raided Harrodsburg. By now, George was a major in the Kentucky County regiment of the Virginia militia. After the Shawnee raid, some of the soldiers from the fort at Harrodsburg went after the Shawnee. George later wrote that the

Kentuckians were lucky they did not find the Indians. The Americans were outnumbered by the Indians and could not afford to lose any men.

George was in charge of the defense of Harrodsburg. For the next few months, the Native Americans and the settlers fought skirmishes. George spent many hours considering what he and the Kentuckians should do. They were surrounded by hostile Indians, who would continue to be armed by the British. He decided to send spies into the Illinois country, which today forms the states of Illinois and Indiana. George wanted to learn about the British defenses in Illinois.

Historians aren't sure if Henry Hamilton bought American scalps from the Northwest Native Americans. What is clear, though, is that some Americans, Europeans, and Indians took scalps from their victims after battles.

Many people have wrongly blamed Native Americans for introducing scalping. Europeans actually did the first scalping in North America. In the 17th century, Dutch leaders paid for Indian scalps. The top part of the head was taken to prove that settlers had killed Native Americans. English colonies also paid for scalps as part of the settlers' effort to take control of Indian lands.

George was already thinking about taking his troops into Illinois, and then north, to attack the British at Detroit. He counted on surprising any British troops he met, since they would not be expecting an American assault. George also hoped he could convince the region's French settlers to support his cause.

George's spies returned to Harrodsburg with good news. The fort at Kaskaskia was not defended by British soldiers. The French militia there was not large, and the French in general could probably be convinced to help the Americans. By taking control of Kaskaskia, the Americans would make it harder for the British to send supplies to the Native Americans. And from that fort, George could take other forts in the region before turning toward Detroit.

In October, George left for Virginia. He needed approval from the leaders in Williamsburg to carry out his plan. Governor Patrick Henry liked George's idea, but he wanted to make sure it stayed secret. The governor did not discuss the plan with the assembly. He also gave George two sets of orders. One set was read in public. It said that George should recruit troops, return to Kentucky, and wait for further orders. George's second set of orders was kept secret. This one gave him the power to raise troops and attack Kaskaskia.

George knew his plan was risky. His troops would be far from home, surrounded by "determined Enemies." But George was ready to fight.

Along with his orders, George received a new rank, lieutenant colonel. He also received money to buy supplies and recruit soldiers. In May 1778, George and his troops headed to Pittsburgh, then traveled down the Ohio River. In Kentucky, George would meet up with more troops that had been recruited there. The soldiers also traveled with 20 settlers and their families, who wanted protection as they headed to Kentucky.

Late in May, the troops stopped at a small island near what is now Louisville. George and his men built a fort, where the settlers planned to stay. On the island, George hoped to train his troops without worrying about Indian attacks. He also hoped that staying on the island would make it difficult for any soldiers to **desert**, or leave without permission. Finally, George told his troops about their secret mission. "Some were alarmed at the thought of being taken so great a distance into the enemy's country," he later wrote. Still, most of the men seemed to support the plan—but not all of them.

A small group of men led by a Lieutenant Hutchins decided to desert rather than fight. The men had found a shallow spot in the river, and before sunrise the next morning, they waded ashore. George sent troops after the deserters, but they only tracked down a few. This search for the deserters delayed the trip to Illinois. Finally, on June 24, George and his left troops for Kaskaskia.

The regiment was smaller than George had hoped. Some of the soldiers he had recruited were not ready to carry out a long march. And leaders in Kentucky had not been able to send as many men as promised. George was leaving for battle with just 178 soldiers. By that time, the men were well trained. And, like George, many already had experience fighting Indians on the frontier.

George thought about attacking Fort Sackville first. It was at Vincennes, in what is now Indiana. This fort was closer than Kaskaskia. But Vincennes also had more Indians nearby. Kaskaskia, George reasoned, would be the easier target.

A few days later, George received news about the situation at Kaskaskia. He and his men met a group of hunters who had just come from the fort. George wrote, "If . . . we could surprise the place, [the hunters] had no doubt of our ability to master it." George was pleased to hear that the French had "horrible ideas of the barbarity of the rebels, especially so of the Virginians." To the French and the Indians, the Americans were the "Big Knives." If the French feared George and his men, it would be easier to defeat them.

George also had another advantage when dealing with the French. A scout had reached the troops as they traveled west. He had good news: France had decided to support the Americans in their fight for independence. The French settlers of the Northwest now might be more likely to turn against the British.

George and his men met hunters, and they joined the regiment as guides. They took a longer route, by land, to avoid British scouts watching the rivers. After a few days, one of the guides seemed lost. Some of the soldiers thought the guide was a spy or traitor. George gave the man one last chance to find the right trail to Kaskaskia. If the guide failed, George would kill him. He could not take any chances with the safety of his men. The guide, though, was not a traitor, just "genuinely bewildered," George later noted. Soon the troops were back on the right path.

On July 4, the regiment was just outside the town of Kaskaskia. George and his men took over a family's house near the Kaskaskia River.

The family told them that the townspeople had suspected an attack a few days before. But now, George wrote, "all was quiet." George led a group of men to the fort, while a larger force went into town. Without firing a shot, George took control of the fort. He then signaled to the other troops. Soldiers who spoke French went through the streets, explaining what was happening. Within a few hours, the town was under complete American control.

George rounded up several citizens to get more information. He also ordered some French militia leaders arrested and put in chains. Slowly, the town filled with a sense of dread. George knew how the people felt about him and his men. The citizens expected the Americans to carry out terrible acts of violence. Instead, George said they were free to do what they liked. His men would not guard them, and they could support the British if they wished. "The scene," George wrote, "changed from an extreme state of dejection to one of great joy."

George had won the people's support by treating them well. He knew the neighboring French villages would soon learn that the Americans could be trusted and treated as friends.

With Kaskaskia firmly under his control, George made plans to attack Cahokia. The town was about 50 miles north, along the Missouri River. The citizens of Kaskaskia, however, told George he didn't have to fight. They could convince the French settlers at Cahokia to accept the Americans as allies. George sent Major Joseph Bowman and some townspeople to Cahokia. George soon learned their mission was a success. He wrote that in Cahokia, "cries of liberty and freedom, and [cheers] for the Americans rang through the whole town." The Americans had taken two towns that had once been under British control and still had not fired their guns.

George soon received more good news. Spain controlled the lands south of Illinois, down to New Orleans. George had sent a spy into this territory, and the spy returned to tell

The Native Americans in the town of Cahokia agreed to support George and the other frontiersmen in the fight against Great Britain.

George that the Spanish were ready to support the Americans in the war. Now George prepared for his biggest target in Illinois: Vincennes.

George led his men through shallow water to the fort at Vincennes in the Kentucky frontier. He captured the fort in February 1779.

Taking—
and Keeping
—Vincennes

George sent spies to Vincennes. The spies entered the fort and pretended to be hunters. They learned that no one in Vincennes had heard about the American victories in Kaskaskia and Cahokia. The spies also came back to George with more good news: British troops were not at the fort. Once again, the Americans would have an easy time taking control.

George prepared to march on Vincennes. As word spread about a possible attack, he received a visit from Father Pierre Gibault, the French priest at Kaskaskia. Gibault wanted to go to

Vincennes before the Americans attacked and talk to the townspeople. George wrote that Gibault "had no doubt of being able to bring [Vincennes] over to the American interest without my being put to the trouble of marching troops against it."

Within a few days, Gibault came through on his promise. He convinced the settlers in Vincennes to support the Americans. The U.S. flag now flew over the largest British fort in Illinois country. George was lucky that neither the French nor the Indians knew how small his forces really were.

In August 1778, George held meetings with chiefs from the Native American tribes near Vincennes. He explained to them why the Americans were fighting the British. He also told the Indians he did not want them to help the Americans. He only wanted them to stop fighting for the British.

At times George acted sternly toward the Indians. One night, some Winnebago tried to kidnap the leader of the Big Knives. George's guards caught the men, and George had them placed in chains. Each day, the other Indians saw the prisoners and George's rough treatment of them.

The chiefs also saw how friendly the French had become with the Americans. Some began to think that perhaps they should side with the Americans, since the French were. Over the next few weeks, about a dozen of the chiefs signed peace treaties with George. Not all the Indians in the region came to these meetings. Some were still eager to help the British. But George had greatly strengthened his position in the Northwest.

While George was meeting with the Indians, new trouble was stirring for the Americans. In Detroit, Governor Hamilton finally heard about the loss of Kaskaskia and Vincennes. He made plans to retake Fort Sackville. He assembled a force of British soldiers and French and

Indian volunteers. In October, the small army left for Illinois.

By this time, George was back in Kaskaskia with his main force. He left a few soldiers and the local Vincennes militia under the command of Captain Leonard Helm. George later wrote, "For some time past we had received no information from Vincennes. . . . we began to feel that something was wrong." George was right to worry—the British were about to capture Vincennes.

When Hamilton reached Vincennes, he first spoke to the French settlers there. He convinced them to put down their weapons and rejoin the British. Then Hamilton turned to Fort Sackville. At the fort, the American commander knew he was in trouble. Helm wrote a letter to George, describing how his scouts never returned with information about the British. "You must think how I feel," Helm wrote, "not four men that I can really depend on, but am determined to act brave."

Bravery, however, was not enough. The British had more men and larger cannons. Helm had no choice. He turned the fort over to Hamilton.

In January, a Spanish merchant who had been in Vincennes reached Kaskaskia. He gave George the news about the American defeat. The merchant also said that in the spring, the British planned to attack the American forces and drive them out of Illinois. Then, with their Indian allies, the British would attack Kentucky as well. George knew he had to act quickly to save his home.

George decided to surprise the British in Vincennes before they could launch their spring attack. They would not expect the Americans to march during the winter.

George combined his forces at Kaskaskia and Cahokia, then recruited a militia. Knowing the rivers of the region would be flooded, George bought a small boat. By placing a few cannons on it, he turned the boat into a warship. Called the *Willing*, the ship sailed on February 4, 1779, with 47 men onboard. The *Willing* carried the Americans' **artillery** and supplies. Two days later, George and about 170 soldiers began to march to Vincennes, where they would meet up with the ship.

The march started off well. The men had to walk through shallow water, but the weather was not too cold. George tried to keep his troops in a good mood. He let them hunt every day and feast every night. Farther along, the men had to wade through deeper water, but they still felt good about their mission. George, however, knew they were in a dangerous spot. "We were now in the enemy's country," he wrote, ". . . with no possibility of retreating in case the enemy should discover and overpower us."

The men began making canoes, in case the *Willing* did not reach them. They would

The men in George's army made canoes to cross the Wabash River on their way to Vincennes.

need the boats to cross the Wabash River and storm Vincennes. On February 20, the Americans found a small boat with five

French hunters onboard. They told George that Hamilton had strengthened his defenses. The hunters also told the Americans about two small boats that were on the river. George's men found one and later used it to cross the Wabash.

When describing the march to Vincennes, George usually tried to make it sound as though everything went well. But the journal of Major Bowman tells a different story. Bowman noted that the volunteers often had to walk in cold rain and wade in water up to their arms. Bowman wrote about the lack of food and worried that some of the men might die from hunger and the cold. Years later, many historians called the march to Vincennes one of the most heroic acts of the American Revolution.

On February 23, 1779, the Americans were just outside Vincennes when they came upon some hunters and took one prisoner. George then gave a note for the man to bring to the people of Vincennes. In it, George described the attack he was ready to launch. He told the citizens who supported the British to head to the fort and prepare for battle. Those on the side of liberty would be taken care of. George later wrote that he hoped the message "would encourage our friends, cause those who were lukewarm to take a decided stand, and astonish our enemies."

That evening, George led the men into town. They easily took control, and some of the citizens welcomed the hungry troops with food. George then sent a small band of men to Fort Sackville.

Inside the fort, Hamilton had heard reports that American troops might be nearby. He had given out bullets and ordered the local militia to stay in the fort. But Hamilton did not really expect an attack. Even when he heard gunshots, Hamilton was not concerned. He thought some Indians were just firing off their rifles in the woods. Then a bullet struck one of his men, and Hamilton realized the fort was under attack.

George, meanwhile, had sent more of his troops to the fort. Hiding behind barns, fences, and houses, they fired on the British from all sides. The men made noises to trick the British into thinking their forces were larger than they really were. From what he knew, Hamilton assumed the Americans had about 500 men. Instead, fewer than 150 were attacking. George later wrote that his men "taunted the enemy in order to provoke them into opening the portholes . . . so that [we] might have the pleasure of cutting them down with [our] rifles."

The American men fired until the next morning. George's men continued to hit any British soldier they could see. The British had less luck shooting the Americans. George sent a note to Hamilton, offering a truce. The British commander refused to

(continued on page 53)

British Lieutenant Governor Henry Hamilton was in Fort Sackville when George's men attacked the fort. George tricked the British into thinking that his forces were larger than they really were.

Hamilton surrendered the British control of Fort Sackville after George told him that additional artillery would soon arrive by boat.

(continued from page 50)

accept it, and the fighting continued. A little later, Hamilton and George met outside the fort. George said he wanted only one thing: a complete British surrender. He explained that his artillery was about to arrive by boat, and then the British would have no chance. Hamilton finally agreed to give up the fort.

While George Rogers Clark and Henry Hamilton debated the truce, a group of Indians came to Vincennes to scout the region. The Indians did not know the Americans were at Vincennes. George's men took them prisoner, and then George had the Indians killed to show the British how determined he was to win. Hamilton called George a butcher. But Hamilton himself had often sent Indians to kill American settlers on the frontier.

George could now turn his attention to the future and capturing Detroit.

George and his men had many confrontations with Native Americans in his effort to protect American settlers from Indian attacks.

Holding the
New Lands

George discussed his plans for attacking Detroit with his officers. Everyone was eager to attack while the British defenses there were weak. But the officers weren't sure the Americans had enough men to successfully take the fort and hold it. George decided to wait until the summer, when he would have more troops to send.

In the meantime, George was busy at Vincennes. He sent Hamilton and other British prisoners to Virginia. Fort Sackville was now called Fort Patrick Henry. The American troops repaired the fort and captured supplies from British ships on the Wabash.

George also met with some of the local Indian tribes, and most promised to remain loyal to the Big Knives. Other tribes including the Delaware and the Shawnee, still attacked the Americans.

Late in March, George and some of his men returned to Kaskaskia. There George learned that a Delaware war party had attacked American traders along the Ohio River. George ordered Captain Helm at Vincennes to go after the Delaware. George wrote that now he had the chance "of showing the other Indians the horrible fate of those who dared to make war on the Big Knives." Helm's men launched a quick, deadly strike against the Delaware.

In Kaskaskia, George kept making plans for his march on Detroit. But he faced several problems. One was getting enough supplies for his troops. The Americans had to borrow money to pay for their supplies. At one point, George had to promise to pay the bills with his own money. George had an even bigger problem. Kentucky and Virginia could not send enough troops for him to take Detroit. He gave up on his plan. Still, the British could never be sure that George and his men might not attack Detroit in the future.

By September 1779, George had returned to Kentucky, eager to build a new fort at the mouth of the Ohio River. More settlers were pouring into the region, and they needed protection. A fort at the Ohio was also important for protecting the new American land in Illinois. At that time, Thomas Jefferson replaced Patrick Henry as governor of Virginia. George's good friend wanted the new fort as well. In January 1780, Jefferson gave George permission to start building. The new fort would be named after Jefferson.

Perhaps the biggest threat to the Kentucky settlers came from the Shawnee. In March, George received a letter from the town of Boonesborough. "We are fully persuaded," the citizens wrote, "that nothing less than a Vigorous **expedition** against the Shawnee Towns will . . . secure the Peace and safety of these Settlements." At the same time, George learned that

Thomas Jefferson was the author of the Declaration of Independence. He was elected governor of Virginia in 1779 and would later serve as president of the United States from 1801 to 1809.

the British were again calling on their Native American allies in Illinois.

When Fort Jefferson was done, George

headed to St. Louis. He talked to the Spanish leaders there, who asked George to help defend the town from nearby Indians. Instead, George went first to Cahokia, to fight Indians threatening that town. After a victorious battle, the Americans took some prisoners. These men told George about a British attack on Kentucky. The British and their Indian allies were heading for Fort Nelson, in Louisville. From there, they could take over the entire region.

George and his men raced back to Fort Jefferson. The British were not far from Fort Nelson. The Indians with them, though, asked to hold off on the attack. Some had heard that George had reached Fort Nelson before them. The Native Americans were not eager to fight the leader of the Big Knives. George's reputation as a great military leader was now well known. The Indians told their British commanders they wanted to attack smaller forts in Kentucky, and the British agreed. Their troops won these battles, then headed back to Detroit with their prisoners.

With Fort Nelson safe, George began to think about fighting the Shawnee. In August 1780, he marched north with an army of about 1,000 troops to battle these Native Americans. The Shawnee knew the Americans were coming. They waited for them at the village of Piqua, in what is now Ohio. The Indians opened fire, and the Americans returned it. After a break, George later wrote, "a heavy firing again commenced, and continued severe until dark, by which time the enemy were totally **routed.**" The American victory angered the Shawnee. Prisoners reported that the Indians planned a massive attack on Kentucky, and Vincennes was also threatened.

In the meantime, the British were attacking in the south. Traveling east to Virginia, George fought briefly under Baron Friedrich von Steuben. This Prussian officer had come to help the Americans win their independence. At Hood's Landing, George led an ambush of British troops. The Americans fought well at first, but the British managed to pull out. After this battle, George returned to the west, and once again thought about Detroit.

In January 1781, George received money from the Virginia Assembly to pay for the Detroit **campaign**. But again he lacked soldiers. Virginia and the Carolinas needed troops to hold off the British. In addition, George could not keep his military plans secret, and the British expected the attack. George went to Kentucky, still hopeful he could find enough men. By the summer of 1781, though, he realized he had to forget about Detroit.

By then, the situation in the Northwest was getting worse. The Americans had abandoned Fort Jefferson, and Vincennes was struggling to survive. The Shawnee and other tribes still posed a threat to Kentucky. Even the end of the Revolution did not completely end the fighting. On October 19, 1781, the British surrendered at Yorktown, Virginia. The British commander in America, General Henry Clinton, was prepared to end all the fighting. But the British commander in Canada wanted to continue to fight.

On October 19, 1781, the war ended when British
General Charles Cornwallis surrendered to General
George Washington at Yorktown, Virginia

General Frederick Haldimand led the British
troops in Canada. He was not ready to let the
Americans take full control of the Northwest.
The general and his officers asked their Indian
allies to raid Kentucky and Illinois. Sometimes
British troops helped carry out these raids.

The raids began in February 1782. The

Americans made things worse when they massacred some Indians along the Ohio River. In June, the Indians fought a bloody battle with American troops, then tortured the U.S. commander in revenge for the American massacre.

Now a general, George was in charge of the Kentucky defense. In August, a large Shawnee force moved on the town of Blue Licks. They surprised the Kentucky soldiers in the area, who were led by Daniel Boone. More than 40 Americans were killed in just a few minutes. Boone later wrote to Virginia asking for help.

Boone and others were angry that George had not been at Blue Licks. He was still at Fort

George and Daniel Boone both settled in Kentucky and often traveled the same lands during the American Revolution. Daniel Boone was one of the first Americans to explore Kentucky, and he founded the town of Boonesborough. He also helped build the "Wilderness Road," an important route through the region. Boone served under George during the last years of the American Revolution. Boone was one of the leaders during the loss at Blue Licks, and he also commanded troops during George's second assault on Piqua.

Daniel Boone, shown here, led a group of Kentucky soldiers in the town of Blue Licks. Over 40 American soldiers were killed there when they were attacked by a group of Shawnee Indians.

Nelson when the Shawnee attacked. The new governor of Virginia, Benjamin Harrison, was also unhappy with George. In response, George planned another large attack on the Shawnee at

Piqua. In November, he set out with about 1,000 troops. When they reached Piqua, the village was almost empty. The Kentuckians burned buildings and took supplies but never fought a major battle with the Shawnee.

Early in 1783, the United States and Great Britain officially agreed to end their fighting. George hoped that the peace would "greatly alter the face of affairs in the back country." The Shawnee did limit their attacks, and most Kentuckians felt safer.

A few months later, George left the military. He was still owed money by Virginia. For five years, he had not received any pay, and he had spent his own money to keep his troops in the field. Settling these money matters would trouble George for many years. Still, he felt good about his accomplishments, and Governor Harrison thanked him for his work. George wrote afterward, "No reward for past services could be so satisfactory to me, as that of the gratitude of my country."

George had spent his entire life as a frontiersman exploring and fighting in the wilderness of Virginia and the Northwest Territory.

The Last Battles

Late in 1783, George traveled to Caroline County, Virginia, to visit his family. About this time, he received a letter from Thomas Jefferson. George's old friend said the British were planning an expedition to explore the West. Jefferson wrote, "How would you like to lead such a party?"

George said no. He was ready to settle down—at least for a little while. He and his soldiers received land for their successful campaign in the Northwest. Now George was in charge of surveying it. He went to Louisville in 1784 and built a home there. He also started the town of Clarksville, in what is now Indiana.

That year, George was given another job. The U.S. government asked him to help make peace with the Native Americans of the Northwest. Even though George had waged war against many Indians tribes, he still wanted peace. He got along well with most Indian leaders. Even some of his old enemies respected him as a warrior. But American leaders only wanted to get as much Indian land as they could.

In 1786, George and two other Americans met with the Shawnee. The Americans used threats to make them agree to peace and give up their land. Once the Shawnee and other tribes signed peace treaties, the U.S. government forced them onto **reservations**. Some Indians did not like the way they were treated by the U.S. government. Once again, they began attacking settlers in Kentucky and Illinois. And once again, the leader of the Big Knives was asked to fight.

In September 1786, about 1,000 Kentucky militia members gathered at Clarksville.

George led them to Vincennes. From there, he would strike against the Indians. The campaign quickly ran into trouble. The troops' supplies took a long time to reach Vincennes. When they did arrive, some of the food had spoiled. Many of the soldiers talked about going home to Kentucky. George went to the troops and asked them to stay. "Only go with me two days march," he said, "[and] if I don't furnish you with as much **provisions** as you want, I will return with you." But many of the men decided to leave. The force that remained was too small to fight. In the spring of 1787, George left Vincennes for the last time.

The Vincennes expedition had lasting effects on George. With his troops desperate for food, George took some supplies from Spanish merchants in Vincennes. Many Kentuckians were upset with Spain at this time. Its troops were taking goods carried on ships along the Mississippi River. Now George believed he had the right to take supplies from the Spanish merchants. They had

In 1787, Congress approved the Northwest Ordinance, which described how the Northwest Territory would be ruled. It applied to lands east of the Mississippi River and north of the Ohio River.

The land was divided into smaller territories that were ruled by governors picked by Congress. As the population grew, the citizens could elect their own lawmakers. Eventually, the territories could become states. Congress outlawed slavery in these lands. The Northwest Territory eventually became the states of Ohio, Indiana, Illinois, Michigan, Wisconsin, and part of Minnesota.

come into America without passports, and George said the men were trading without permission. His taking the supplies upset Spain and some Americans.

One of these Americans was a Kentucky general named James Wilkinson. He was also a secret agent for Spain. He demanded that George be punished. He also began to write letters that attacked George's behavior. One of the Spanish merchants from Vincennes took George to court. George already had legal problems because of his debts. Now he was in deeper trouble.

George also had a personal problem. When he returned to Kentucky, he began to drink. He struggled with his alcohol problem for the rest of his life. In 1791, Thomas Jefferson wrote a letter to a Kentucky judge. He said that if George had not started drinking, he could have done more great things. If George could beat his **addiction**, "his lost ground might yet be recovered." After reading this letter, George wept.

As he fought all his troubles, George still looked for new land. He talked to Spain about settling land in Mississippi. Later, he made plans to help France fight Spain in North America. In return, he and his men would receive land. The U.S. government did not want Americans fighting Spain, so George never left for this battle.

After his military career ended, George had plenty of time for his hobbies and to host guests.

George lived a quiet life, and his youngest brother William looked after him. In 1804, William and Meriwether Lewis went on their famous trip to explore the West. During this time, George's health began to fail. He was still drinking, and his legal problems had not ended. He owed money, and Virginia refused to repay

After his military career ended, George had time to study the plants and wildlife in Kentucky.

George the money he spent during the Revolution. He had to give his land to his family, so he would not lose it in court.

The fearless man who once led troops into battle faced a painful end. In 1809, he fell into his fireplace and burned himself badly. Part of his right leg had to be removed. He also suffered a stroke, which made it hard for him to speak and use his right hand. Once in a while George still left his log cabin. But most of his time, he was alone. He suffered two more strokes, and the third one killed him on February 13, 1818.

People seemed to have forgotten George during his last years. But during the 20th century, Americans rediscovered his bravery during the Revolution. In 1936, President Franklin D. Roosevelt attended the opening of the George Rogers Clark Memorial. This building in Vincennes, Indiana, honors the man who made the "Old Northwest" part of America.

GLOSSARY

addiction–constant use of harmful drug that leads to illness.

allies–people or armies that help others fight a battle.

ambushed–attacked by hidden soldiers.

artillery–large guns, such as cannons.

campaign–a military mission.

crucial–extremely important.

desert–leave an army without permission.

expedition–a trip to explore land or fight a military battle.

frontier–the outer edges of settled lands.

militia–group of citizens who serve as soldiers during an emergency.

plantations–large farms mostly in the southern part of the United States.

provisions–food and water needed for a military campaign.

regiment–a group of soldiers.

reservation–land set aside by the U.S. government for Native Americans.

routed–beaten badly in a battle.

skirmishes–small battles with just a few soldiers taking part.

slaughter–extremely bloody murder.

survey–to measure the boundaries of land.

CHRONOLOGY

1752   Born on November 19, in Albemarle County, Virginia.

1757   Moves with family to Caroline County.

1772   Leaves on a surveying trip down the Ohio River.

1773   Farms land in West Virginia.

1774   Fights Native Americans during Dunmore's War.

1775   Arrives in Kentucky.

1776   Leads efforts to make Kentucky part of Virginia; buys gunpowder for local militia.

1777   Defends Harrodsburg; leaves for Virginia to get permission to attack British forts in the Northwest.

1778   Leads Kentucky troops westward into Illinois; takes control of Kaskaskia, Cahokia, and Vincennes.

1779   Launches sneak attack to recapture Vincennes from the British; puts off planned attack on Detroit; returns to Kentucky.

1780   Defeats Shawnee at Piqua.

1781   Tries again to organize forces for an attack on Detroit but fails.

1782   Leads another attack on the Shawnee at Piqua.

1783   Leaves the military with the rank of brigadier general.

1786   Serves at peace talks with Shawnee; briefly returns to Vincennes but does not fight.

1809   Loses leg after falling into a fire.

1818   Dies on February 13, outside Louisville, Kentucky.

REVOLUTIONARY WAR TIME LINE

1765	The Stamp Act is passed by the British. Violent protests against it break out in the colonies.
1766	Britain ends the Stamp Act.
1767	Britain passes a law that taxes glass, painter's lead, paper, and tea in the colonies.
1770	Five colonists are killed by British soldiers in the Boston Massacre.
1773	People are angry about the taxes on tea. They throw boxes of tea from ships in Boston harbor into the water. It ruins the tea. The event is called the Boston Tea Party.
1774	The British pass laws to punish Boston for the Boston Tea Party. They close Boston harbor. Leaders in the colonies meet to plan a response to these actions.
1775	The battles of Lexington and Concord begin the American Revolution.
1776	The Declaration of Independence is signed. France and Spain give money to help the Americans fight Britain. Nathan Hale is captured by the British. He is charged with being a spy and is executed.
1777	Leaders choose a flag for America. The American troops win some important battles over the British. General Washington and his troops spend a very cold, hungry winter in Valley Forge.
1778	France sends ships to help the Americans win the war. The British are forced to leave Philadelphia.

1779	French ships head back to France. The French support the Americans in other ways.
1780	Americans discover that Benedict Arnold is a traitor. He escapes to the British. Major battles take place in North and South Carolina.
1781	The British surrender at Yorktown.
1783	A peace treaty is signed in France. British troops leave New York.
1787	The U.S. Constitution is written. Delaware becomes the first state in the Union.
1789	George Washington becomes the first president. John Adams is vice president.

FURTHER READING

Flanagan, Alice K. *The Shawnee.* New York: Children's Press, 1998.

Kozar, Richard. *Daniel Boone and the Exploration of the Frontier.* Philadelphia: Chelsea House, 2000.

Lee, Susan and John. *George Rogers Clark: War in the West.* Chicago: Children's Press, 1975.

Moore, Kay. *If You Lived at the Time of the American Revolution.* New York: Scholastic, 1998.

Stefoff, Rebecca. *First Frontier.* New York: Benchmark Books, 2001.

PICTURE CREDITS

INDEX

ABOUT THE AUTHOR

MICHAEL BURGAN was an editor at *Weekly Reader,* where he created educational material for an interactive, online service and wrote about current events. Michael is now a freelance author and a member of the Society of Children's Book Writers and Illustrators. His books include biographies of President John F. Kennedy, Secretary of State Madeleine Albright, and astronaut John Glenn; two volumes in the series American Immigration; and short books on the Boston Tea Party, the Declaration of Independence, the Bill of Rights, and the New Deal. Michael has a BA in history from the University of Connecticut.

Senior Consulting Editor **ARTHUR M. SCHLESINGER, JR.** is the leading American historian of our time. He won the Pulitzer Prize for his book *The Age of Jackson* (1945), and again for *A Thousand Days* (1965). This chronicle of the Kennedy Administration also won a National Book Award. He has written many other books, including a multi-volume series, *The Age of Roosevelt.* Professor Schlesinger is the Albert Schweitzer Professor of the Humanities at the City University of New York, and has been involved in several other Chelsea House projects, including the Colonial Leaders series of biographies on the most prominent figures of early American history.